Little

D0766429

COOKBOOK

The Family Circle Promise of Success

Welcome to the world of Confident Cooking, created for you in the
Family Circle Test Kitchen, where recipes are double-tested by our team
of home economists to achieve a high standard of success.

M U R D O C H   B O O K S®
Sydney • London • Vancouver • New York

POPULAR AUSTRALIAN FOOD

Many of the interesting terms which describe uniquely Australian cuisine are inherited from the early pioneers and bushmen who moved from place to place carrying their swag and billy can.

Anzac Biscuits: Made with rolled oats, coconut, flour, sugar, golden syrup, butter, bicarbonate of soda and water. They were made and sent in tins to Australian soldiers at the battlefields during World War I.

Meat Pies: Individual mince meat pies small enough to be held in your hands for eating. They are traditionally sold at sporting and other community events, usually smothered with tomato sauce.

Balmain Bugs: Unusually shaped flat crustaceans found in Sydney harbour. They have a mild-flavoured white flesh and are usually barbecued, grilled or boiled.

Billy Tea: Tea made in a metal can, called a billy, over an open fire. The billy has a wire handle and a tight-fitting lid. Water is brought to the boil, the lid removed and tea added. The billy is then removed from the fire and tea drunk from metal cups.

Cocky's Joy: A tin of either golden syrup or treacle was one of the basics that swagmen used to carry with them. It had many uses like sweetening billy tea, spreading on damper or pouring over puddings.

Cuppa: A cup of tea.

Damper: A basic bread originally made simply with flour and water, kneaded, shaped into a round and cooked in the coals of a fire made on the ground. Raising agents or self-raising flour are used to make damper now. Some campers make the dough and mould a small amount around one end of a thick stick. The stick is then held over a fire. When the damper is cooked, golden syrup is poured in the hole left by the stick.

Fish: Australia's coastline is a breeding ground for a large variety of fish. Snapper, garfish,

leatherjacket, jewfish, flathead, and gemfish are some of the most common types available. John Dory and Barramundi, both mild-flavoured fish, are very popular and highly regarded.

Granny Smith Apples: Green-skinned variety with crisp juicy flesh. They were first grown in Sydney, New South Wales in the late nineteenth century. They are used extensively in cookery and are an excellent eating apple.

Jumbuck: Young sheep.

Lamingtons: Pieces of light sponge cake dipped in chocolate icing and coconut. It is believed Queenslanders named them after a popular early Governor of Queensland.

Rock Oysters: Popular edible molluscs found on Australian seashores. Eaten straight from the shell, although some people prefer them grilled or poached.

Pavlova: Basically a large meringue served with fruit and cream. Controversy still surrounds the country of origin. Australians claim it as their very own and believe it was invented by a chef in Western Australia when

the great Russian dancer Pavlova was touring early this century. New Zealanders claim it had already been written into their cookery books ten years earlier.

Shellfish: Australians are quite partial to shellfish. In seafood restaurants, a platter consisting of a variety of shellfish and fish is highly prized.

Tucker: Colloquial term for food.

Tropical Fruits: When in season, fruits such as mangoes, paw paws and pineapples are sent from northern Australia to southern states and are enjoyed in various ways.

Vegemite: A vegetable extract used as a spread on toast or bread and as a flavouring in soups and casseroles. Australians who live overseas have a reputation for not being happy unless they have a supply of vegemite.

Add bacon, onion and garlic to hot oil in pan. Stir over medium heat for 3 minutes.

Add tomato and worcestershire sauces, stock and mixed herbs. Bring to boil.

Using a sharp knife, cut shortcrust pastry into eight 14 cm diameter circles.

Place puff pastry circles over top of pies, press edges to seal. Trim pastry edges.

MEAT, CHICKEN & SEAFOOD

Most Australian meals have as their main ingredient, meat, chicken or seafood. The quality of Australian produce is high, so even a simple meal of grilled chops and vegetables is a culinary treat.

Meat Pies with Tomato Sauce

Preparation time:
30 minutes
Total cooking time:
30 minutes
Makes 8

1 tablespoon oil	1 tablespoon
2 rashers bacon,	worcestershire sauce
finely chopped	2 cups beef stock
1 medium onion,	1/2 teaspoon dried
finely chopped	mixed herbs
1 clove garlic, crushed	4 sheets ready-rolled
500 g beef mince	shortcrust pastry
2 tablespoons plain	1 egg yolk, lightly
flour	beaten
2 teaspoons dry	4 sheets ready-rolled
mustard powder	puff pastry
1/4 cup tomato sauce	tomato sauce,
	extra, for serving

1. Preheat oven to moderately hot 210°C (190°C gas). Heat oil in pan, add bacon, onion and garlic, stir over medium heat for 3 minutes.
2. Add beef to pan, stir over high heat for 3 minutes or until meat is well browned. Add flour and mustard powder, stir 1 minute. Add tomato and worcestershire sauces, stock and mixed herbs. Bring to boil, reduce heat. Simmer, uncovered, 5 minutes or until mixture has reduced and thickened, stirring occasionally. Allow mixture to cool.

3. Using a plate or bowl as a guide, cut shortcrust pastry into eight 14 cm diameter circles. Line eight 11 cm pie tins. Divide cooled filling evenly into pastry shells. Brush around pastry rim with beaten yolk.
4. Using a plate as a guide, cut puff pastry into eight 12 cm diameter circles. Place over tops of pies, press edges to seal, trim pastry edges. Decorate if desired. Brush tops with yolk. Using a sharp, pointed knife, make 2 small slits in top of each pie. Place tins on a baking tray, bake 15 minutes or until golden. Serve hot pies with extra tomato sauce.
Note: Meat Pies may be served with mashed potato or deep-fried chips.

Carpetbag Steak

Serve with a salad.

Preparation time:
25 minutes
Total cooking time:
10–20 minutes
Serves 4

4 beef eye fillet steaks, 4 cm thick	*freshly ground black pepper*
12 shelled oysters	*2 tablespoons oil*
2 tablespoons chopped fresh parsley	*1 cup beef stock*
2 teaspoons lemon juice	*2 teaspoons worcestershire sauce*
	60 g butter, chopped

1. Using sharp knife, cut a deep pocket into side of each steak.
2. Combine oysters, parsley, lemon juice and pepper in a bowl. Spoon into steak pockets and secure with toothpicks.
3. Heat oil in pan; add steaks. Cook over high heat 2 minutes each side, turning once. For rare steaks, cook each side 1 more minute. For medium and well done, reduce heat to medium, continue cooking 2–3 minutes each side for medium and 4–6 minutes each side for well done. Drain on paper towels.
4. Bring stock and sauce to boil in pan. Reduce heat, stir in butter until melted. Serve with steaks.

Carefully cut a deep pocket into the side of each fillet steak.

Spoon combined oysters, parsley, lemon juice and pepper into pockets.

Remove cooked steaks from pan and drain on paper towels.

Reduce heat. Add chopped butter to mixture in pan. Stir until butter melts.

Surf 'n' Turf

For seafood lovers.

Preparation time:
20 minutes
Total cooking time:
15–20 minutes
Serves 4

LEMON MUSTARD SAUCE	
30 g butter	*2 teaspoons Dijon*
1 spring onion, finely	*mustard*
chopped	
1 clove garlic, crushed	*2 tablespoons oil*
1 tablespoon plain	*1 large green lobster*
flour	*tail (or 2 small*
1 cup milk	*tails), shelled*
2 tablespoons cream	*4 beef scotch fillets*
1 tablespoon lemon	*170 g can crab,*
juice	*drained*

1. To make Lemon Mustard Sauce: Heat butter in medium pan; add onion and garlic. Stir over medium heat 1 minute or until onion is soft. Add flour, stir over low heat 1 minute.
2. Add milk gradually to pan, stirring until mixture is smooth. Stir constantly over medium heat until mixture boils and thickens; simmer 1 minute. Remove from heat, stir in cream, lemon juice and mustard; keep warm.

3. Heat oil in pan; add lobster tail. Cook over medium heat 3 minutes each side or until just cooked through. Remove from pan, keep warm.
4. Add steaks to pan, cook over high heat 2 minutes each side to seal, turning once. For rare steaks, cook each side 1 more minute. For medium and well done steaks, reduce heat to medium, continue cooking 2–3 minutes each side for medium and 4–6 minutes each side for well done. Drain on paper towels. To serve, place steaks on plates, top with crab then sliced lobster. Pour Lemon Mustard Sauce over and garnish with spring onion.

Add flour to butter mixture in pan, stir over low heat for 1 minute.

Remove pan from heat and stir in cream, lemon juice and mustard. Keep warm.

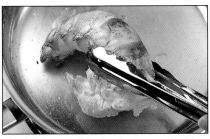

Cook lobster tail for 3 minutes each side or until just cooked through.

Cook steaks over high heat for 2 minutes each side to seal, turning once.

Rissoles with Gravy

Preparation time:
25 minutes
Total cooking time:
10 minutes
Serves 4

---

500 g beef mince
1 onion, finely
  chopped
1 clove garlic,
  crushed
2 tablespoons tomato
  sauce
1 teaspoon dried
  mixed herbs
1 egg, lightly beaten
1 cup fresh
  breadcrumbs

2 tablespoons oil

GRAVY
2 tablespoons plain
  flour
2 cups chicken stock
1 tablespoon tomato
  paste
2 tablespoons
  chopped fresh
  parsley

---

1. Place beef, onion, garlic, tomato sauce, herbs, egg and breadcrumbs in a bowl. Mix with hands until well combined.
2. Divide mixture into 8 portions and shape into patties.

3. Heat oil in large, heavy-based pan; add rissoles 4 at a time. Cook over high heat for 1 minute each side, turning once. Reduce heat to medium, cook for 2 minutes each side or

until cooked through. Remove rissoles from pan, drain on paper towels; keep warm.
4. To make Gravy: Blend flour with chicken stock and tomato paste in a small jug until mixture is smooth. Add to pan juices, stir over medium heat for 3 minutes or until gravy boils and thickens. Strain, stir in chopped parsley. Serve with rissoles.

HINT
You can vary the flavour of rissoles by using a variety of herbs. Chopped fresh oregano, parsley or basil blend well with the tomato sauce. Freshly grated parmesan cheese may be added to mixture.

Using your hands, mix mince, onion, garlic, sauce, herbs, egg and crumbs.

Divide mixture into 8 portions and shape into round patties.

Cook rissoles, over medium heat, for another 2 minutes each side.

Add gravy mixture to pan juices, stir over medium heat until gravy boils and thickens.

Kangaroo Steaks with Red Wine Sauce

Preparation time:
20 minutes +
2 hours marinating
Total cooking time:
10 minutes
Serves 4

1 cup good quality dry red wine	*1 small onion, finely chopped*
1 teaspoon chopped fresh chives	*500 g loin kangaroo fillet or 4 kangaroo fillet steaks*
1 clove garlic, crushed	*1 tablespoon oil*
	1/2 cup cream

1. Combine wine, chives, garlic and onion in bowl. Add kangaroo meat, toss until coated. Cover with plastic wrap. Refrigerate for at least 2 hours or overnight. Remove meat from marinade, drain. Reserve marinade.
2. Heat oil in pan; add meat. Cook over high heat 2 minutes to seal sides, turning. For rare meat, cook 2 more minutes. For medium meat, reduce heat to medium, continue cooking for 3 minutes. (If using steaks cook for 3–4 minutes, turning occasionally.)
3. Remove meat from pan. Cover and keep warm. Add reserved marinade and cream to pan juices, bring to boil. Reduce heat to low and simmer uncovered 3 minutes or until sauce has reduced and thickened.
4. Slice cooked fillets thinly and serve with warm sauce. Serve with mashed sweet potato and steamed sugar snap peas.
Note: Loin fillet is more readily available than steaks. Kangaroo meat has a very low fat content and will become dry if overcooked. Cook it to rare or medium stage only and leave for a few minutes before serving. This will produce tender, juicy kangaroo meat.

Toss kangaroo meat in marinade until it is well coated.

Cook meat over high heat for 2 minutes. Turn to ensure all sides are sealed.

Remove cooked meat from pan. Add reserved marinade and cream to pan.

Slice kangaroo fillets thinly for serving. Serve with warm sauce.

Leg of Lamb with Gravy

Simple to carve.

Preparation time:
25 minutes
Total cooking time:
1¼–1¾ hours +
20 minutes standing
Serves 6

1.5 kg leg of lamb, tunnel-boned	*1 egg, lightly beaten*
2 tablespoons oil	*½ teaspoon grated lemon rind*
STUFFING	*GRAVY*
1 cup fresh breadcrumbs	*2 tablespoons plain flour*
1 small onion, finely chopped	*1½ teaspoons worcestershire sauce*
1 clove garlic, crushed	*2 cups chicken stock*
2 tablespoons chopped fresh parsley	

1. Preheat oven to moderate 180°C. Trim lamb of excess fat and sinew.
2. To make Stuffing: In a small bowl, combine the breadcrumbs, onion, garlic, parsley, egg and rind. Press stuffing mixture into cavity of the lamb.
3. Tuck in ends of lamb to enclose stuffing. Tie lamb securely with string at regular intervals to retain shape during cooking. Place oil in a deep baking dish and add the prepared lamb. Bake 1–1¼ hours for rare meat, 1¼ –1½ hours for medium, or 1½–1¾ hours for well-done. Remove lamb from pan, and leave, covered, for 10–15 minutes before slicing.
4. To make Gravy: Drain all except ¼ cup of pan juices from baking dish. In a small jug, blend flour, worcestershire sauce and stock, stirring until smooth. Add to juices in dish, stir over medium heat 3 minutes or until the gravy boils and thickens; strain. Serve with sliced lamb.

Using a sharp knife, trim lamb of excess fat and sinew.

In a small bowl, combine breadcrumbs, onion, garlic, parsley, egg and rind.

Tuck in ends of lamb and tie lamb securely with string at regular intervals.

Add blended ingredients to juices in baking dish and stir until smooth.

Curried Lamb Chops

Preparation time:
15 minutes
Total cooking time:
50 minutes
Serves 4

---

8 lamb chump chops
2 tablespoons oil
2 onions, sliced
2 cloves garlic,
 crushed
1 tablespoon curry
 powder
1 tablespoon plain
 flour

425 g can tomatoes
1¹/₂ cups water
1/4 cup fruit chutney
2 large carrots, cut
 into 1 cm slices
2 tablespoons
 chopped fresh
 parsley, for serving

1. Trim meat of excess fat and sinew. Heat oil in heavy-based pan; add chops. Cook over medium-high heat for 2 minutes each side or until well browned; drain on paper towels.
2. Add onion and garlic to pan, stir 2 minutes or until soft. Add curry powder and flour, stir 1 minute.
3. Return chops to pan with undrained, crushed tomatoes, water, chutney and carrots; bring to boil.
4. Reduce heat, simmer, covered, 40 minutes or until chops are tender, stirring occasionally. Sprinkle with parsley.

Using a sharp knife, trim lamb chops of excess fat and sinew.

Stir onion and garlic until soft. Add curry powder and flour and stir for 1 minute.

Return drained chops to pan. Add tomatoes, water, chutney and carrots.

Cover and simmer over low heat until chops are tender. Stir occasionally.

Lamb's Fry and Bacon

Preparation time:
20 minutes
Total cooking time:
10–15 minutes
Serves 4

---

500 g lamb's fry
plain flour
salt and pepper
30 g butter
1 tablespoon oil
2 onions, sliced
4 rashers bacon,
chopped

1½ cups chicken
stock
1 teaspoon
worcestershire sauce
2 tablespoons
chopped fresh
parsley, for serving

---

1. Peel off the outer membrane of lamb's fry with your fingers and discard. Cut lamb's fry into 1 cm slices. Dust with seasoned flour; shake off excess flour and reserve 2 tablespoons.
2. Heat butter and oil in frying pan; add onion. Stir over medium heat for 2 minutes or until soft. Remove onion from pan, set aside.
3. Add bacon to pan, stir over medium heat for 2 minutes or until crisp; remove from pan, set aside.
4. Add lamb's fry to pan, cook over medium-high heat for 1 minute each side or until lightly browned, turning once. Return onion to pan. In a jug, blend chicken stock, worcestershire sauce and reserved flour. Pour into pan, bring to boil. Reduce heat to low, simmer for 3 minutes or until lamb's fry is tender and sauce has thickened. Stir in cooked bacon, heat through. Serve immediately sprinkled with fresh parsley.

> **HINT**
> Lamb's fry should be pink in centre when cooked. It will become tough if overcooked. Serve Lamb's Fry and Bacon for breakfast with toast or as a main meal with mashed potatoes and steamed green beans, peas or broccoli.

Dust lamb's fry slices with seasoned flour. Shake off excess. Reserve 2 tablespoons.

Add sliced onion to butter and oil in frying pan. Stir over medium heat until soft.

Add chopped bacon to pan and stir until bacon is crisp. Drain on paper towels.

Return onion to pan. Pour in blended stock, sauce and reserved flour.

Bushman's Breakfast

Preparation time:
15 minutes
Total cooking time:
20 minutes
Serves 2

2 lamb loin chops	*1 large tomato, cut in*
2 thick sausages	*half*
2 rashers bacon	*2 tablespoons grated*
100 g mushrooms,	*cheddar cheese*
sliced	*1 tablespoon oil*
	2 eggs

1. Trim chops of excess fat. Pierce sausages all over with a fork.
2. Place chops and sausages on oiled grill tray, cook under high heat 2 minutes; turn, cook 2 minutes. Continue cooking chops and sausages until they are done to your liking.

3. In a pan, fry bacon until crisp, remove; keep warm. Add mushrooms, cook briefly. Keep warm. After 4 minutes of cooking time, place tomato, cut-side down, on grill tray. Cook for 2 minutes, turn. Sprinkle cheese on top. Cook until tender.
4. About 3 minutes before serving, heat oil in frying pan. Cook eggs over low heat. Serve with cooked meat, tomato, bacon and mushrooms.

Pierce sausages all over with a fork. Trim chops of excess fat.

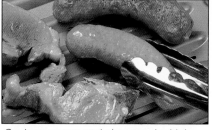

Cook sausages and chops under high heat for 2 minutes, turn, cook 2 minutes.

Cook tomato halves, cut-side down, for 2 minutes. Sprinkle cut side with cheese.

Heat oil in a frying pan. Break eggs into pan and cook eggs over low heat.

Battered Saveloys

Preparation time:
25 minutes
Total cooking time:
10–15 minutes
Makes 8

---

8 thick wooden
   skewers
8 saveloys or
   frankfurts
plain flour
oil for deep frying
tomato sauce

BATTER
1/4 cup self-raising
   flour
2 tablespoons plain
   flour
1/4 teaspoon
   bicarbonate of soda
1/2 cup water
1 egg, lightly beaten

---

1. Insert wooden skewers through centre of saveloys lengthways, leaving about 8 cm protruding at one end for a handle. Dust saveloys lightly with flour.

2. To make Batter: Place flours, soda, water and egg in food processor or blender. Process mixture for 10 seconds or until all ingredients are combined and the mixture is free of lumps. Transfer mixture to a bowl.

3. Heat oil to moderately hot in deep heavy-based pan. Holding end of skewers, dip saveloys one or two at a time into batter. Use a spoon, if necessary, to coat saveloys completely; drain off excess batter.

4. Holding skewer ends, gently lower battered saveloys into oil. Hold for a few seconds until saveloys float unaided. Cook for 1 minute or until lightly golden and crisp. Carefully remove from oil with tongs or slotted spoon, drain on paper towels.

Repeat process with remaining saveloys. Re-dip each cooked saveloy in remaining batter and repeat the cooking process. Place tomato sauce in a bowl and place on the table for dipping.

Insert thick wooden skewers through the centre of saveloys lengthways.

Process mixture until all ingredients are combined and mixture is free of lumps.

Dip saveloys into batter. Use a spoon, if necessary, to coat saveloys completely.

After initial cooking, re-dip each saveloy in batter and repeat the cooking.

23

Balmain Bugs with Mango sauce

Preparation time:
  10 minutes
Total cooking time:
  5 minutes
Serves 4

8 large green balmain bugs or 2 large green lobster tails	2–3 tablespoons sour cream
	1/4 cup lemon or lime juice
MANGO SAUCE	1 teaspoon soft brown sugar
1 large or 2 small mangoes	2–3 teaspoons Thai sweet chilli sauce

1. Lower bugs into large pan of lightly salted boiling water. Simmer, uncovered, for 4–5 minutes or until shells have changed to an orange-red colour.
2. Gently separate the heads from the bodies. Use a pair of sharp kitchen scissors to cut along the soft underside of the bugs.
3. Pull shell apart and ease out the flesh. Cut each piece of flesh in half lengthways.
4. To make Mango Sauce: Peel mango, remove seed and roughly chop flesh. Place flesh in food processor. Add sour cream, juice, sugar and sauce. Process for 20–30 seconds or until smooth. Refrigerate, covered, until required. If sauce is too thick add a little extra cream or juice. Serve Balmain Bug meat on bed of mixed salad leaves with extra slices of fresh mango and Mango Sauce for dipping.

Note: As an alternative to Mango Sauce, combine 1/2 cup sour cream, 1 tablespoon worcestershire sauce, 2 tablespoons tomato paste, 1 teaspoon horseradish cream and 1/2 teaspoon French or German mustard. If fresh mango is unavailable, use tinned mango slices or 170 g can mango puree.

Using tongs, lower bugs into large pan of lightly salted boiling water.

To peel, separate the heads from the bodies and cut along the underside.

Gently ease the flesh away from the shell and cut each piece in half lengthways.

Place mango pieces, sour cream, juice, sugar and sauce in food processor.

25

Oysters Mornay

Oyster lover's treat.

Preparation time:
15 minutes
Total cooking time:
5–10 minutes
Serves 4

---

20 g butter
1 tablespoon finely
chopped chives
2 teaspoons plain
flour
1/2 cup milk
2 tablespoons grated
cheddar cheese

24 oysters in half
shell
1/3 cup fresh
breadcrumbs
crushed rock salt for
serving

1. Heat butter in a small pan, add chopped chives, stir over medium heat 1 minute. Add flour, stir over low heat 1 minute. Add milk gradually to pan, stirring until the mixture is smooth.
2. Stir constantly over medium heat 1 minute or until mixture boils and thickens. Lower heat, simmer, stirring, 1 minute. Remove from heat, stir in grated cheese.
3. Spoon cheese sauce over oysters, sprinkle with the fresh breadcrumbs.
4. Place oysters on a grill tray. Cook under high heat 2 minutes. Serve with rock salt.

Add milk gradually to pan, stirring continuously until the mixture is smooth.

Remove pan from heat and stir in the grated cheese.

Spoon small amounts of sauce over each
oyster and sprinkle with breadcrumbs.

Place oysters on a grill tray and cook
under high heat for 2 minutes.

Barbecued King Prawns

A wonderful lunch.

Preparation time:
20 minutes
+ marinating
Total cooking time:
3 minutes
Serves 4

1.25 kg green king prawns	2 tablespoons lemon juice
1/4 cup fresh parsley sprigs	1 tablespoon honey
1/4 cup oil	2 cloves garlic, crushed
2 tablespoons barbecue sauce	2 tablespoons chopped fresh chives

---

1. Peel king prawns leaving tails intact; devein.

2. Finely chop parsley. Place in a bowl and combine with oil, sauce, juice, honey, garlic and chives.

3. Add prawns, stir until combined. Cover, refrigerate at least 4 hours or overnight.

4. Cook prawns on a preheated barbecue grill for 3 minutes or until just cooked through, turning once.

Note: If preferred, prawns can be cooked under a preheated grill or in a shallow pan over high heat. May be served with a sliced fresh bread stick and green salad.

Peel the green king prawns leaving tails intact; devein.

Using a sharp knife, finely chop the fresh parsley sprigs.

Add prawns to marinade mixture and stir until combined. Cover and refrigerate.

Cook prawns on a preheated barbecue grill for about 3 minutes, turning once.

Roast Chook with Baked Vegetables

Preparation time:
25 minutes
Total cooking time:
1 hour
Serves 4

1.4 kg chicken	2 tablespoons lemon
6 medium potatoes	juice
375 g pumpkin	2 rashers bacon,
4 small onions	rind removed
30 g butter, melted	2 tablespoons oil

1. Preheat oven to moderate 180°C. Trim chicken of excess fat and sinew. Rinse the chicken and pat dry with paper towels. Peel potatoes, pumpkin and onions. Cut potatoes in half and pumpkin into even-sized pieces.
2. Combine melted butter and lemon juice and brush some of the mixture around inside of chicken. Fold wings back behind chicken; tie legs together with string. Brush chicken all over with the remaining butter mixture. Place on a rack in a large baking dish.
3. Cut bacon rashers into strips, lay across chicken breasts. Place the prepared vegetables in a smaller baking dish. Brush vegetables all over with oil.
4. Place both dishes in oven. Bake for 1 hour or until juices run clear when chicken thigh is pierced with a skewer and vegetables have turned golden and are tender in the centre. Serve with steamed broccoli and green beans.

> **HINT**
> Baked potatoes are delicious if, before baking, you boil them for 5 minutes, drain, pat dry and then score across them with the prongs of a fork. Place in dish and brush all over with a little olive oil which has been mixed with a clove of crushed garlic.

Using a sharp knife, cut potatoes in half and pumpkin into even-sized pieces.

Fold wings back behind the chicken. Tie chicken legs together with string.

Place all the vegetables in a smaller baking dish and brush vegetables with oil.

Chicken is cooked if juices run clear when you pierce thigh with a skewer.

Using a 20 cm round cake tin as a guide, mark a circle in the cornflour on tray.

Add caster sugar gradually, 1 tablespoon at a time, beating until mixture is thick.

Spread or pipe meringue onto circle on tray. Smooth top with a flat-bladed knife.

Spread cream over top of cooled pavlova. Decorate with strawberry halves.

DESSERTS

Australians love to finish off their meal with a dessert. Fresh fruits often feature, both raw and cooked. Ice-cream and cream are the most popular accompaniments.

Strawberry Pavlova

A traditional dish.

Preparation time:
20 minutes
Total cooking time:
1 hour 15 minutes
+ cooling
Serves 6

---

2 teaspoons cornflour	*1 teaspoon vinegar*
4 egg whites	*1¼ cups thick cream*
¾ cup caster sugar	*250 g strawberries,*
1 teaspoon vanilla	*halved*
essence	

---

1. Preheat oven to very slow 120°C. Brush a 32 x 28 cm baking tray with melted butter or oil. Line base with paper; grease paper. Dust lightly with sifted cornflour, shake off excess. Using a 20 cm round cake tin or pan lid as a guide, mark a circle in the centre of prepared tray. Place egg whites in a small, dry mixing bowl. Using electric beaters, beat for 1 minute or until soft peaks form.

2. Add the caster sugar gradually, 1 tablespoon at a time, beating constantly until mixture is thick and glossy and all the sugar has dissolved. Add vanilla essence and vinegar, beat until combined.

3. Spread or pipe meringue onto marked circle on prepared tray. Bake 1¼ hours or until pale and crisp. Cool completely on the tray in the oven, with door slightly ajar. When pavlova is cool, slide a flat-bladed knife underneath and carefully ease pavlova onto a serving plate.

4. Place cream in medium mixing bowl. Using electric beaters, beat cream until stiff peaks form. Spread over top of cooled pavlova. Place strawberry halves decoratively on top of cream. Passionfruit pulp may be spooned over strawberries and cream if desired.

HINT
Although strawberries are often served with pavlova, other fruits can be used. Try sliced kiwi fruit, mango, banana or a combination of your favourite fruits or berries. Grated chocolate may be sprinkled over the top.

Banana Custard

A delicious treat.

Preparation time:
15 minutes
Total cooking time:
5 minutes
Serves 4

---

2 bananas
1 egg, lightly beaten
2 tablespoons
   custard powder
2 tablespoons sugar
1 cup milk
1/2 cup thick cream

2 tablespoons
   desiccated coconut,
   toasted (optional)
1/2 teaspoon ground
   cinnamon
   (optional)

---

1. Slice banana diagonally.

2. Combine beaten egg, custard powder, sugar, milk and cream in medium, heatproof bowl and whisk until mixture is smooth.

3. Place the bowl over a pan of simmering water. Stir mixture constantly for 5 minutes or until custard thickens slightly and coats the back of a wooden spoon.

4. Remove bowl from heat and gently stir in the sliced banana. Serve sprinkled with coconut and cinnamon if desired.

Note: For variety, custard may be flavoured with a few drops of almond or vanilla essence.

Using a sharp knife, slice bananas diagonally.

Whisk combined egg, custard powder, sugar, milk and cream until smooth.

Stir constantly until custard thickens slightly and coats back of wooden spoon.

Remove bowl from heat and gently stir in the sliced banana.

Lemon Delicious

Self-saucing pudding.

Preparation time:
20 minutes
Total cooking time:
1 hour
Serves 4

---

60 g butter
3/4 cup caster sugar
3 eggs, separated
1 teaspoon grated
lemon rind

1/3 cup self-raising
flour, sifted
1/4 cup lemon juice
3/4 cup milk
icing sugar for dusting

---

1. Preheat oven to moderate 180°C. Brush a 1-litre capacity ovenproof dish with oil. Using electric beaters, beat butter, sugar, egg yolks and rind in small bowl until mixture is light and creamy. Transfer to a medium bowl.
2. Add flour. Using a wooden spoon, stir until just combined. Add juice and milk; stir to combine.

3. Place egg whites in small, dry bowl. Using electric beaters, beat until firm peaks form. Add to flour mixture. Using a metal spoon, fold in until just combined.
4. Spoon into dish. Place dish in a deep baking dish. Pour in boiling water to come one-third of the way up sides of dish. Bake 1 hour. Spoon some sauce on each serving.

Beat butter, sugar, egg yolks and rind until mixture is light and creamy.

Add juice and milk to mixture and stir with a wooden spoon until combined.

Using a metal spoon, gently fold beaten egg whites into flour mixture.

Pour boiling water into baking dish until it comes one-third of the way up sides.

Baked Apples and Cream

Preparation time:
20 minutes
Total cooking time:
45 minutes
Serves 4

---

4 Granny Smith
  apples
1/3 cup sultanas
2 tablespoons soft
  brown sugar
1/2 teaspoon ground
  mixed spice

30 g butter, cut into
  pieces
1 cup orange juice or
  water
2/3 cup whipped cream
  for serving

1. Preheat oven to moderate 180°C. Using an apple corer, remove cores. Replace a small amount of core in bases of the apples. Using a sharp knife, make a shallow cut through the skin, around the middle of the apples to prevent skin from bursting during cooking.
2. Combine sultanas, sugar and spice.

Spoon into apples.
3. Place apples in small baking dish; add butter and pour in juice or water.
4. Bake, uncovered, 45 minutes, basting occasionally. Remove from oven; cool for 5 minutes. Place apples on individual serving plates. Pour pan juices over apples. Serve with whipped cream.

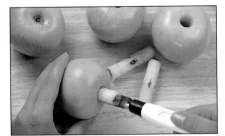

Remove cores from apples. Replace a small amount of core in bases of apples.

Combine sultanas, sugar and spice. Spoon some mixture into each apple.

Place apples in baking dish, add pieces of butter. Pour juice or water into dish.

Allow apples to cool for 5 minutes. Place on serving plates. Pour pan juices over.

Lemon Meringue Pie

Preparation time:
 40 minutes
Total cooking time:
 15–20 minutes
Serves 8

½ x 340 g packet
 shortcrust pastry
 mix

LEMON FILLING
1 cup sugar
½ cup cornflour
2 teaspoons grated
 lemon rind

1½ cups water
¾ cup lemon juice
60 g butter, chopped
3 egg yolks

MERINGUE
3 egg whites
½ cup caster sugar

---

1. Preheat oven to moderately hot 210°C (190° gas). Prepare pastry according to instructions on packet. Roll pastry out thinly to cover base and sides of a 23 cm pie plate. Cut a sheet of greaseproof paper large enough to cover pastry-lined dish.

Spread a layer of dried beans or rice over paper. Bake 7 minutes, remove from oven, discard paper and beans. Return pastry to oven for another 7 minutes or until lightly golden. Cool.
2. To make Lemon Filling: Combine sugar, cornflour and lemon rind in pan. Blend in water and lemon juice, stir until smooth. Stir over medium-high heat for 2 minutes or until mixture boils and thickens.
3. Add butter, stir over heat for 1 minute or until butter has melted. Remove from heat, quickly add egg yolks, whisk until combined; cool. Spread Lemon Filling evenly into the prepared pastry shell.
4. To make Meringue: Place egg whites in small dry bowl. Using electric beaters, beat until soft peaks form. Add sugar gradually, beating until mixture is thick and glossy and sugar has dissolved. Spread over Lemon Filling. Bake 5 minutes. Remove, cool.

Spread a layer of dried beans or rice evenly over paper in dish.

Add water and lemon juice to pan and stir until mixture is smooth.

Add butter to pan and stir over heat for 1 minute or until butter has melted.

Spread meringue mixture roughly over Lemon Filling using a flat-bladed knife.

Dumplings & Cocky's Joy

Preparation time:
  15 minutes
Total cooking time:
  15 minutes
Serves 4

1½ cups self-raising
  flour
2 tablespoons caster
  sugar
60 g butter, melted
1 egg, lightly beaten
¼ cup milk

1⅓ cups water
⅓ cup golden syrup
½ cup soft brown
  sugar
½ teaspoon lemon
  juice
60 g butter, extra

---

1. Sift flour into mixing bowl. Add sugar, stir until combined. Make a well in the centre.
2. Combine butter, egg and milk. Add mixture to dry ingredients. Using a knife, stir until just combined.

3. Combine water, syrup, sugar, juice and extra butter in large pan. Stir over high heat until sugar has dissolved, bring to boil.
4. Carefully drop heaped tablespoonsful of the flour mixture into syrup. Reduce heat to low and cover pan. Cook for 10 minutes or until dumplings have risen and are cooked through. Ladle the syrup over dumplings occasionally during cooking.

Sift flour into bowl. Add sugar and stir to combine. Make a well in the centre.

Combine butter, egg and milk. Add to dry ingredients and stir with a knife.

Place water, syrup, sugar, juice and extra butter in pan. Stir until sugar dissolves.

Drop heaped tablespoonsful of flour mixture into syrup. Reduce heat, cover.

Combine flours and sift 3 times onto greaseproof paper.

Transfer egg mixture to a large bowl. Add flours and use a metal spoon to fold in.

Pour cream into medium bowl and beat until stiff peaks form.

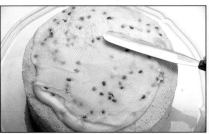

Using a flat-bladed knife, spread prepared icing over top of sponge.

TEATIME TREATS

With a cup of tea or coffee, these treats are enjoyed by all Australians. Children love to find lamingtons or Anzac Biscuits in their school lunch-boxes.

Passionfruit Sponge

Preparation time:
20 minutes
Total cooking time:
15–20 minutes
Makes one 20 cm cake

⅓ cup cornflour
⅓ cup plain flour
⅓ cup self-raising flour
4 eggs
2 teaspoons finely grated lemon rind
⅔ cup caster sugar

¾ cup thick cream

PASSIONFRUIT ICING
1¼ cups icing sugar
15 g butter
2 tablespoons passionfruit pulp

---

1. Preheat oven to moderate 180°C. Brush 2 shallow 20 cm round cake tins with melted butter or oil. Line bases with paper; grease paper. Dust tins lightly with flour, shake off excess. Sift combined flours 3 times onto greaseproof paper.
2. Using electric beaters, beat eggs and lemon rind in a small bowl for 5 minutes or until thick and pale.

Add sugar gradually, beating constantly until mixture is pale yellow and glossy. Transfer mixture to large bowl. Using a metal spoon, fold in flours quickly and lightly. Spread mixture evenly in prepared tins. Bake for 15 minutes or until sponges are lightly golden and shrink from sides of tins. Leave sponges in tins for 2 minutes

before turning onto a wire rack to cool.
3. Using electric beaters, beat cream in medium mixing bowl until stiff peaks form. Spread cream evenly over 1 sponge layer. Place remaining sponge on top.
4. To make Passionfruit Icing: Combine icing sugar, butter and pulp in heatproof bowl. Stand bowl in pan of simmering water and stir until icing is smooth and glossy; remove from heat. Spread icing over top of sponge using a flat-bladed knife.

HINT
When you are making sponge cakes, it is important to gently fold the flour into egg mixture. If you try to beat the flour in, the texture will become thick and heavy.

Lamingtons

Truly Australian.

Preparation time:
1 hour
Total cooking time:
1 hour
Makes 25

1½ *cups self-raising flour*	ICING
⅓ *cup cornflour*	4 *cups icing sugar*
185 g *butter, softened*	⅓ *cup cocoa powder*
1 *cup caster sugar*	30 g *butter, melted*
2 *teaspoons vanilla essence*	⅔ *cup milk, extra*
3 *eggs, lightly beaten*	3 *cups desiccated coconut, approximately*
½ *cup milk*	
¾ *cup thick cream*	

1. Preheat oven to moderate 180°C. Brush a shallow 23 cm square cake tin with melted butter or oil. Line base and sides with baking paper. Sift flour and cornflour into large bowl. Add butter, sugar, essence, eggs and milk.

2. Using electric beaters, beat on low speed 1 minute or until ingredients are just moistened. Beat mixture on high for 3 minutes or until mixture is free of lumps and increased in volume. Pour mixture into prepared tin; smooth surface. Bake 1 hour or until skewer comes out clean when inserted in centre of cake. Leave cake in tin for 3 minutes before turning onto wire rack to cool.

3. Using a serrated knife, trim top of cake until flat. Trim crusts from sides of cake. Cut cake in half horizontally. Using electric beaters, beat cream in small mixing bowl until stiff peaks form. Place first layer of cake on a board, spread evenly with cream. Place remaining cake layer on top. Cut cake into 25 squares.

4. To make Icing: Sift icing sugar with cocoa. Combine with butter and milk in medium heatproof bowl. Stand bowl over pan of simmering water, stirring until icing is smooth and glossy; remove from heat. Place 1 cup of coconut on a sheet of greaseproof paper. Using 2 forks, roll a piece of cake in chocolate icing; hold cake over bowl, allow excess to drain. Roll cake in coconut, place on wire rack. Repeat with remaining cake, add extra coconut for rolling as needed.

HINT
Lamingtons are easier to make if you cook the cake a day in advance. This means the cake will not crumble when you are cutting it into squares.

Add butter, sugar, essence, eggs and milk to sifted flours in bowl.

Beat mixture on high speed until it is free of lumps and has increased in volume.

Using a serrated knife, carefully cut cake in half horizontally.

Hold cake with 2 forks and roll in icing. Allow excess icing to drain back into bowl.

Caravel Slice

Rich and delicious.

Preparation time:
20–30 minutes
Total cooking time:
25 minutes
Makes 15

¾ cup desiccated
   coconut
1 cup self-raising
   flour
½ cup caster sugar
125 g butter, melted

FILLING
400 g can condensed
   milk

30 g butter, extra
2 tablespoons golden
   syrup

TOPPING
150 g dark chocolate,
   chopped
20 g white vegetable
   shortening (copha)

---

1. Preheat oven to moderate 180°C. Brush a 28 x 18 cm shallow oblong cake tin with melted butter or oil. Cover base with baking paper, extending over 2 sides. Combine coconut, flour and sugar in medium bowl; add butter, stir until well combined. Press into prepared cake tin. Bake for 15 minutes or until golden brown.
2. To make Filling: Combine milk, extra butter and syrup in medium pan, stir over medium heat until boiling. Lower heat, continue stirring for 5 minutes. Remove from heat, spread over base in tin. Bake for 10 minutes. Remove and cool.
3. To make Topping: Place chocolate and shortening in medium heatproof bowl. Stand over pan of simmering water, stir until the chocolate has melted and is smooth.
4. Spread evenly over caramel filling and allow to set. Cut into squares using a warm knife.

HINT
Popular for morning or afternoon tea. May be cut into smaller squares for serving after dinner with tea or coffee.

Using the back of spoon, press mixture into base of prepared tin.

Lower heat and continue stirring mixture, using a wooden spoon, for 5 minutes.

Stand bowl over pan of simmering water, stir until mixture is smooth.

Using a warm knife, cut into squares. Use a ruler as a guide.

Vanilla Slice

A custard treat.

Preparation time:
40 minutes
Total cooking time:
15 minutes
Makes 9

---

2 sheets ready-rolled
  puff pastry
1 cup caster sugar
3/4 cup cornflour
1/2 cup custard
  powder
3 cups milk
1 cup cream
60 g butter

2 teaspoons vanilla
  essence
3 egg yolks
1 1/2 cups icing sugar
1/4 cup passionfruit
  pulp
2 teaspoons lemon
  juice
15 g butter, extra,
  softened

---

1. Preheat oven to hot 240°C (200°C gas). Brush 2 oven trays with oil. Line base and sides of a shallow 23 cm square cake tin with aluminium foil, extending over 2 sides. Place pastry sheets on prepared oven trays. Prick all over with a fork. Bake 8 minutes or until golden. Remove from oven; trim each pastry sheet to 23 cm square. Place 1 sheet in prepared tin, top side down.
2. Combine sugar, cornflour and custard powder in medium pan. Gradually add milk and cream; stir until smooth. Stir mixture constantly over medium heat 2 minutes or until mixture boils and thickens. Add the butter and essence; stir until smooth.
3. Remove from heat. Whisk in egg yolks until combined. Spread custard over pastry in tin, cover with remaining pastry, top side down; cool.
4. Combine icing sugar, passionfruit pulp, juice and butter in heatproof bowl. Stand bowl over pan of simmering water and stir until icing is smooth and glossy; remove from heat. Lift slice out of cake tin. Spread icing over top of slice; allow to set.

Place pastry sheets on trays and use a fork to prick pastry sheets all over.

Slowly add milk and cream to pan and stir until smooth.

Remove pan from heat. Whisk in egg yolks until well combined.

Spread icing over top of slice. When set, cut into squares using serrated knife.

Anzac Biscuits

Quick and easy.

Preparation time:
20 minutes
Total cooking time:
20 minutes
Makes about 25

1 cup plain flour	*1 tablespoon golden*
1 cup rolled oats	*syrup*
3/4 cup desiccated	*1 1/2 teaspoons*
coconut	*bicarbonate of soda*
3/4 cup caster sugar	*2 tablespoons boiling*
125 g butter	*water*

1. Preheat oven to slow 150°C. Brush 2 oven trays with melted butter or oil. Place flour, oats, coconut and sugar in a large mixing bowl, stir until combined.
2. Combine butter and golden syrup in small pan, stir over high heat until melted. Mix soda with boiling water, add to melted butter and syrup. Add to flour mixture, stir until combined.
3. Shape level tablespoonsful of mixture into balls and flatten slightly; place onto prepared trays, about 6 cm apart.
4. Bake 15–20 minutes or until crisp and golden. Remove from oven, stand 2 minutes. Loosen biscuits and cool on wire rack.

Using a wooden spoon, combine flour, oats, coconut and sugar in a bowl.

Add butter mixture to bowl and stir until well mixed.

Place flattened balls onto prepared trays about 6 cm apart.

After 2 minutes, remove biscuits from trays and place on a wire rack.

Neenish Tarts

An old favourite.

Preparation time:
1 hour
Total cooking time:
15 minutes
Makes 18

---

2 sheets ready-rolled
   shortcrust pastry
1 tablespoon plain
   flour
1/2 cup milk
2 egg yolks
60 g butter
2 tablespoons caster
   sugar

1/4 teaspoon vanilla
   essence

ICING
1 cup icing sugar
2 tablespoons milk,
   extra
1 tablespoon cocoa
   powder

---

1. Preheat oven to moderately hot 210°C (190°C gas). Using a fluted 7 cm cutter, cut pastry into 18 circles. Press circles into shallow patty tins; prick evenly with a fork. Bake 10 minutes or until lightly golden.
2. Blend flour and milk in pan until smooth. Stir over medium heat for 2 minutes until mixture boils and thickens. Remove from heat, quickly stir in yolks until smooth. Cover with plastic wrap; cool. Using electric beaters, beat butter, sugar and essence in bowl until light and creamy. Add egg mixture gradually, beat until smooth. Spoon into pastry shells and smooth the tops.
3. To make Icing: Combine sugar and milk in heatproof bowl. Place bowl over pan of simmering water, stir until smooth and glossy; remove from heat. Transfer half of icing to small bowl, add cocoa; stir until smooth.
4. Using a small, flat-bladed knife, spread plain icing over half of each tart starting from the centre and making a straight line with the icing, then pushing icing out to the edge. Allow to set. Reheat chocolate icing and ice other half of each tart.

When you have pressed pastry circles into tins, prick pastry evenly with a fork.

Using electric beaters, beat butter mixture until quite smooth.

With bowl sitting over pan of simmering water, stir mixture until smooth and glossy.

When plain icing has set, ice the other half of each tart with chocolate icing.

Rocky Road

Sticky pieces of fun.

Preparation time:
20 minutes
Total cooking time:
3 minutes
Makes about 20

---

375 g milk chocolate, coarsely chopped	**200 g glacé cherries, coarsely chopped**
1/2 cup desiccated coconut	**250 g pink and white marshmallows, halved**
1 cup unsalted peanuts	

---

1. Line a 28 x 18 cm shallow oblong tin with baking paper.
2. Place chocolate in large heatproof bowl. Stand bowl over a pan of simmering water, stir until chocolate has melted and is smooth. Remove from heat and cool slightly.
3. Add coconut, peanuts and chopped cherries, stir until combined. Add marshmallows, stir until combined.
4. Spread mixture into paper-lined tin. Allow to stand until chocolate has set. When set, use a sharp knife to cut Rocky Road into small squares.
Note: Rocky Road can be made with dark chocolate or chocolate melts.

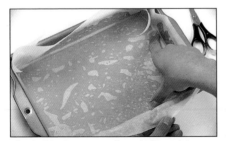

Cut baking paper to fit a shallow oblong tin and line tin.

Stir chocolate with a wooden spoon until chocolate has melted and is smooth.

Add halved marshmallows to mixture and stir until evenly distributed.

Using a spoon, spread mixture into prepared tin. Leave until chocolate is set.

White Christmas

A festive tradition.

Preparation time:
15 minutes
Total cooking time:
2 minutes
Makes 35 squares

---

3 cups Rice Bubbles
1 cup desiccated
   coconut
3/4 cup powdered
   milk
1/2 cup icing sugar
60 g mixed glacé
   fruit, chopped

60 g red and green
   glacé cherries,
   chopped
1/4 cup sultanas
125 g white vegetable
   shortening (copha)
125 g white chocolate
   melts

---

1. Brush a 28 x 18 cm shallow oblong tin with oil. Line base and sides with paper.

Combine Rice Bubbles, coconut, powdered milk, icing sugar, glacé fruit, cherries and sultanas, in a large bowl.

2. Chop shortening; place in heatproof bowl with chocolate. Stir over a pan of simmering water until mixture is melted and smooth.

3. Combine chocolate and Rice Bubble mixture. Press into prepared tin and refrigerate until set.

4. Remove from tin. Allow to stand for 10 minutes before cutting into squares for serving.

Combine Rice Bubbles, coconut, powdered milk, sugar and fruits in a bowl.

Place shortening in bowl with chocolate. Stir over pan of simmering water.

Add chocolate mixture to Rice Bubbles mixture and stir until combined.

Use a sharp knife to cut mixture into squares for serving.

Pumpkin Scones

Homestead fare.

Preparation time:
15–20 minutes
Total cooking time:
15 minutes
Makes about 15

2½ cups self-raising
   flour
¼ teaspoon dried
   mixed herbs
60 g butter, chopped
1 egg, lightly beaten

1 cup cooked, mashed
   pumpkin (350 g
   raw pumpkin)
1–2 tablespoons milk
milk, extra, for
   glazing

---

1. Preheat oven to moderately hot 210°C (190°C gas). Brush a 28 x 18 cm shallow oblong tin with melted butter or oil. Sift the flour into a large mixing bowl. Stir in mixed herbs; add chopped butter. Using fingertips, rub butter into the flour for 2 minutes or until mixture is fine and crumbly.

2. Combine beaten egg, mashed pumpkin and milk. Add to flour mixture and stir with a knife until just combined.

3. Turn dough onto lightly floured surface. Knead for 10 seconds or until smooth. Press mixture out gently to form a round, about 2 cm thick. Cut the mixture into rounds

using a floured 5 cm cutter.

4. Place rounds in prepared tin and brush tops with extra milk. Bake for 15 minutes or until tops are lightly golden. Turn onto a wire rack to cool. Serve warm or cold with butter.

HINT
If you prefer sweet scones, you can replace herbs with 2 teaspoons of sugar. Pumpkin Scones are easy and quick to make and delicious for a snack. Sometimes they are used as a substitute for bread – serve buttered with soup or main course. They are best cooked in the hottest part of the oven and eaten on the day they are made.

Rub butter into flour, using your fingertips, until mixture is fine and crumbly.

Stir flour and pumpkin mixture with a knife until ingredients are just combined.

Using a floured 5 cm cutter, cut dough into rounds before placing into tin.

Using a pastry brush, brush tops of dough with extra milk.

Damper with Cocky's Joy

Preparation time:
20 minutes
Total cooking time:
25 minutes
Makes one damper

---

3 cups self-raising flour
1–2 teaspoons salt
90 g butter, melted
1/2 cup water
1/2 cup milk

milk, extra, for glazing
flour, extra, for dusting
butter, extra, for serving
golden syrup

---

1. Preheat oven to moderately hot 210°C (190°C gas). Brush an oven tray with melted butter or oil. Sift flour and salt into large mixing bowl; make a well in the centre. Combine butter, water and milk and add to flour. Stir with a knife until just combined.

2. Turn onto lightly floured surface; knead 20 seconds or until smooth. Transfer dough to tray; press out to a 20 cm round.

3. Using a sharp pointed knife, score into 8 sections 1 cm deep. Brush with milk; dust with flour. Bake for 10 minutes.

4. Reduce heat to moderate 180°C. Bake 15 minutes or until damper is golden and sounds hollow when tapped. Serve with extra butter and syrup.

Add combined butter, water and milk to dry ingredients in bowl. Stir with a knife.

Knead dough on floured surface for 20 seconds or until smooth.

Score dough with a sharp pointed knife into 8 sections about 1 cm deep.

Bake damper until it is golden and sounds hollow when tapped.

INDEX